whales, seals, and caribou. In other places, they fished, gathered wild plants, and hunted animals such as buffalo and deer. They killed animals not for sport but for food, shelter, and clothing.

Christopher Columbus arrived in the Americas in 1492. Let's take a look at what life was like in North America just a short time before Columbus got here. We'll have to step back into what we call "pre-Columbian" times, more than 500 years ago, to meet the first Americans. If you're ready to time-travel, let's go!

▲ **MANY SCIENTISTS** believe that the first people came to North America from Asia about 12,000 years ago or earlier by walking over a strip of land called the Bering Land Bridge. Others think people came by boat. Over time, people settled everywhere from Alaska to the tip of South America.

CHECK IT OUT!

When the Ice Age ended, the land bridge connecting Asia and North America disappeared. Do you know why?

Do you know why Native Americans are called Indians?

Sea People of the Pacific Northwest

In 1492, the rivers and oceans of the Pacific Northwest were filled with salmon, halibut, and many other fish. Along the shore, people dug for clams and mussels. The area got lots of rain. Tall cedar trees grew in the forests. So did bushes full of tasty berries. Many

THE HEAD WHALER stands tall in the cedar canoe. He plunges his harpoon deep into the whale's side. Long ropes attached to the harpoon help the men follow the wounded whale. The whalers tow the dying whale to shore, where their families wait to welcome them home.

MAKAH SEA HUNTERS depended on their harpoons. The tip of the harpoon had a large mussel-shell blade. Harpoons also had two sharp barbs made of elk bone or antler.

▼ **THE MAKAH HAD** canoes of all sizes. Some whaling canoes were 46 feet long and could hold a dozen or more men. War canoes could be even larger. Smaller one-person canoes were used for river fishing and short trips at sea.

◄ **THE MAKAH LIVED** in five villages on the Pacific coast in what is now Washington State. The biggest was Ozette, near the tip of the Olympic peninsula. People lived in family groups. Families differed in status, or importance. There were "royal" families and common families. Each family had a leader, and the most powerful of the family leaders acted as chief. Within the family, each person was also ranked by importance. There were rules about how people of different ranks should behave.

America 1492

KIDS DISCOVER

RED WHITE & BLUE CORN

GAMES THE IROQUOIS PLAYED

GIANT HAIRY ELEPHANTS

IN PARTNERSHIP WITH
Houghton Mifflin Harcourt.

The First Americans

The very first Americans were big-game hunters who carried spears of bone and stone. They came from Asia, but they weren't looking for a new place to live. They were following the giant buffalo and woolly mammoth. They tracked and killed those animals to survive. In North America, they found beavers as big as bears, but no jets roared though the skies, and no car horns honked. There were no towns, cities, highways, or shopping malls. The forests were dense and untouched. In parts of the continent, it is said, a squirrel could go hundreds of miles jumping from tree to tree without ever touching the ground.

Over thousands of years, the first Americans developed many ways to live on the land. Some settled along the coasts. Others came to live in forests, on plains, or in cliff houses in the deserts. Wherever they lived, they used the land's natural resources wisely.

By 1492, most first Americans hunted and farmed for a living. In the Arctic, they hunted

THE FIRST AMERICANS lived in small groups and moved often, always searching for big game. Capturing such large animals required skill and luck. Sometimes, animals could be chased into swamps, where they sank into mud and were trapped. At other times an animal might be speared and wounded. Then the hunters tracked it until it died.

▲ THE GROUND SLOTH didn't eat meat. Instead it used its front legs to pull leaves from trees for breakfast, lunch, and supper. This beast was over 18 feet long – more than three times the height of an average adult man. It weighed three tons, about as much as three small cars. Its giant back legs and tail supported its huge body.

▼ ICE AGE HUNTERS chipped away flakes of rock until a stone had a sharp edge. Then they took a straight stick that had been peeled and smoothed. They tied the sharpened stone to one end of the stick and made a spear.

THE WOOLLY MAMMOTH was a 10-foot-tall, four-ton elephant. It roamed North America during the Ice Age. Its cousin, the imperial mammoth, which lived on the Great Plains, was even bigger – over 13 feet tall. Mammoths had long, shaggy, reddish-brown outer coats and thick, woolly undercoats. Their fur kept them warm in freezing blizzards. Each mammoth tooth was twice as big as a brick. The shiny tusks of ivory curved upward.

of the people in the Pacific Northwest farmed, but they didn't need to grow crops to stay alive. They could catch dinner by hook, net, or spear.

One group of Native Americans living in the Pacific Northwest in 1492 was the Makah. Their villages faced the Pacific Ocean. They hunted sea otters, seals, and whales. Every spring, gray whales and fur seals swam by as they made their way to cold northern waters. When the Makah saw the whales, they got ready for the hunt. The last whaling canoe is about to leave. Hop aboard for a ride.

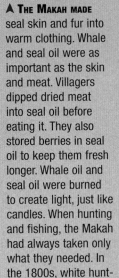

▲ **THE MAKAH MADE** seal skin and fur into warm clothing. Whale and seal oil were as important as the skin and meat. Villagers dipped dried meat into seal oil before eating it. They also stored berries in seal oil to keep them fresh longer. Whale oil and seal oil were burned to create light, just like candles. When hunting and fishing, the Makah had always taken only what they needed. In the 1800s, white hunters killed so many fur seals that the seals almost died out.

◄ **THE MAKAH FOUND** many uses for the cedar trees from nearby forests. They made the wood into fishhooks, boxes, bowls, and canoe paddles. Whaling canoes were carved from cedar trees. Women wove the bark into skirts, baskets, mats, and ropes.

◄ **THE MAKAH** didn't just eat the whale's meat and throw the rest away. The barnacles that attached themselves to the whale's skin made a very tasty treat. The Makah turned whalebone and tissue into fishing line and tools of all kinds. They made containers from the whale's intestines. And they used and traded whale oil, which was very valuable.

◄ **WOULD YOU LIKE** to go to a party where everyone came home with a great gift? At a special ceremony called a potlatch, a host showed the social standing of his or her family. Dressed in fancy robes (left), hosts gave their guests a huge meal and beautiful presents, such as fine blankets, carved boxes, and even canoes. The most important guests got the best gifts.

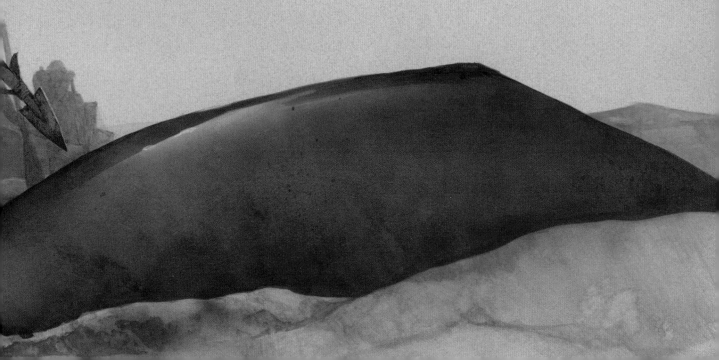

6

Peoples of the Desert Southwest

Little rain falls in the Southwest. Some parts are desert. The rest is very dry. When rain does come, it often pours down in short, strong thunderstorms that cause flash floods. This climate doesn't seem like a very good place for people, especially for farmers. Yet Native Americans of the Southwest were expert farmers, grow-

◀ **PUEBLO PEOPLES** lived in the area we now call the Southwest. The Hopi made their home in what is now northeastern Arizona. The Hopi traded with other peoples, including those of Mexico. Some of the things they traded for were parrot feathers, copper, and turquoise.

▲ **THIS HOPI WOMAN** was photographed in 1906. She wears the ancient "squash blossom" hairstyle of her people. Women wore it when they were old enough to get married.

▲ **HOPI WOMEN MADE** the pottery and baskets they used as trays, serving platters, and corn containers. Some bowls had a snake design on them. The snake was a symbol of lightning and rain.

▲ **SOUTHWESTERN** corn comes in six colors. For the Hopi, yellow corn stood for the north, blue corn for the west, red corn for the south, and white corn for the east. Purple corn stood for the sky and gray corn for the underworld. The Hopi ate corn at every meal. Popcorn was a Hopi treat.

➤ **KACHINAS WERE** powerful spirits that played a big part in the lives of the Hopi. People wearing different kachina masks gave prayers to the kachina spirits for good harvests. Hopi girls were given dolls that were carved and dressed to look like kachinas. These dolls helped the children learn about the different kachina spirits.

ON THIS DAY, ONE OF the men is looking to see how well his young corn plants are growing. In a Hopi village, men did most of the farming.

ing crops of corn, beans, squash, and cotton.

The Hopi were one group of Pueblo people living in the Southwest in 1492. Like some other Pueblo peoples, they lived in multi-story buildings or houses. These were built on the tops of mesas (high, flat-topped hills). They were also built on the sides of cliffs. Put on your hiking boots and climb the long, winding stone stairway to the top of the mesa. The people of the pueblo are waiting there to meet you.

MOST PUEBLOS stood two or three stories high. The bottom floors had no doors or windows, so attackers couldn't get in. People could enter these rooms only through a hole in the roof or in the floor above.

Pueblos were made of stone that was covered with sun-baked clay called adobe. There were 75 to 600 or more rooms in a village. As new people came, builders simply added new rooms to the old ones.

◄ THE HOPI SOCIETY is matrilineal – people trace their ancestry through their mother's family. Several families form clans. The oldest woman is the leader of daily life. Her brother is the leader of ceremonies and rituals. Each pueblo had a kiva – a special underground room that only men and boys could enter. Secret ceremonies were held in the kiva.

THE HOPI PRACTICED what is called dry farming. They captured every bit of water available. One of the ways they did this was to plant seeds deep in sand that had rock beneath it. As the plant grew, its roots soaked up water left in the ground from rains or flash floods. The rock kept the water from draining away.

Farmers of the Great Plains

The western Great Plains is a flat, dry area. Tall grasses once grew everywhere there. In 1492, high winds whipped across the plains, carrying dirt or the flames of fast-moving lightning fires. Winters were very cold, but summers sizzled. More rain fell in the eastern parts of the Great Plains.

Five hundred years ago, few Native Americans lived all year on the Great Plains. Many peoples were nomadic, following buffalo herds. They hunted on the plains in warm weather but wintered in the mountains or woodlands that bordered the plains. One group that did live on the plains was the Mandan people. The women raised corn, squash, beans, and sunflowers. The men hunted bear, deer, rabbits, and other animals. Their most important prey was the buffalo, which grazed in the tall grasses. Every spring and fall, the Mandan tracked the buffalo across the plains. One hunt has already started. Clouds of dust are rising in the distance. A buffalo herd must be near. Let's catch up with these hunters from long ago.

◄ THE MANDAN lived in large domed houses called earth lodges. A rounded frame of branches was covered with earth to keep the lodge warm in winter and cool in summer. Some lodges housed several families and their animals. Women owned the lodges. When a Mandan man married, he moved into his wife's lodge. Each Mandan village had its own government. There was a general council, and two members were chosen for special leadership. One was a skilled warrior. The other had skills for keeping the peace. Another member took care of day-to-day governing.

◄ EVERY SUMMER the Mandan held a four-day celebration called Okipa. Men wearing buffalo skins and masks did dances that copied the movements of the animals they hunted. Older people told stories of the Mandan past. Young men took part in tests of strength and courage.

◄ THE MANDAN LIVED along the banks of the Missouri River in present-day North Dakota. Plains culture stretched from Alberta, Canada, to the Texas Panhandle. The Mandan traded vegetables and other goods with the nomadic Plains peoples, who did not grow their own food.

BUFFALO DANCER

▲ IT'S EARLY FALL. The Mandan are on the plains hunting buffalo. On this day, they're using a plan called a buffalo jump. Wearing a buffalo skin as a disguise, the hunt leader walks ahead of the herd, trying to lead it toward a cliff's edge. Other hunters walk behind the herd. When the leader gives the signal, all the hunters stamp

Why do you think the Mandan made their homes along the Missouri River?

◄ **THE MANDAN** used buffalo hides to make bull boats for river travel. They did this by stretching the hides over a tub-shaped framework of willow tree branches. A bull boat could carry several people.

their feet, make loud noises, and wave torches to frighten the buffalo. The scared animals run straight over the edge of the cliff and fall to their death.

➤ **BUFFALO HUNTERS** used dogs to carry supplies. The goods were placed on a pack made of a small skin frame tied to two poles. One end of each pole was tied to the dog's shoulders. The other ends trailed on the ground. Dogs could carry up to 75 pounds on the frame – but they could also decide to run away to chase a rabbit!

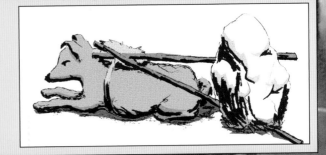

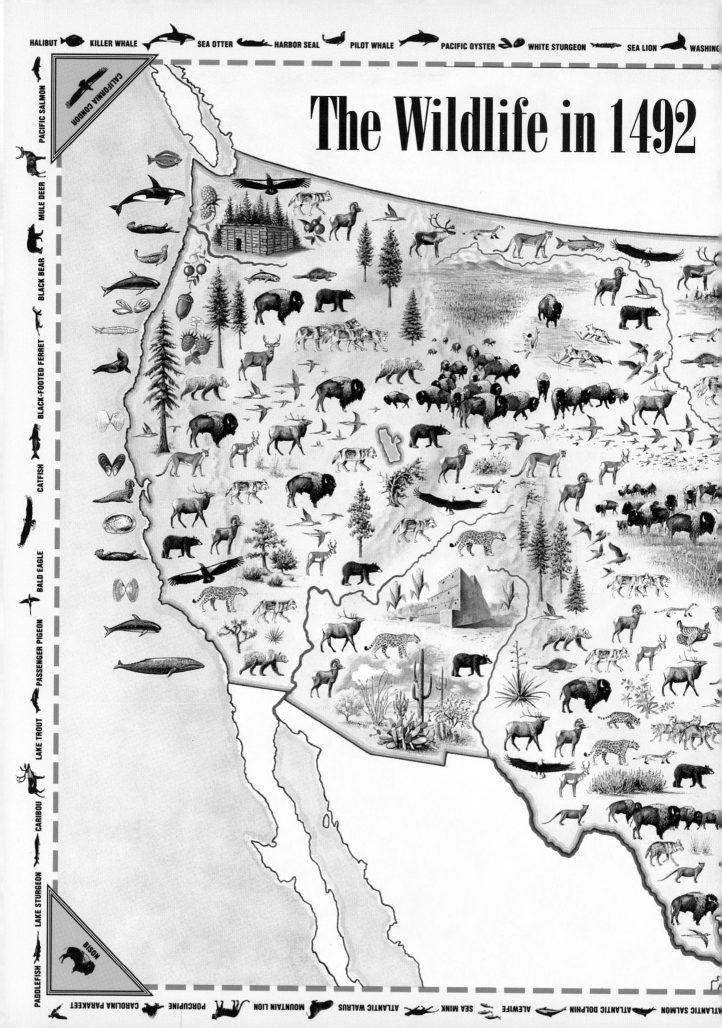

The Wildlife in 1492

HALIBUT   KILLER WHALE   SEA OTTER   HARBOR SEAL   PILOT WHALE   PACIFIC OYSTER   WHITE STURGEON   SEA LION   WASHING

CALIFORNIA CONDOR

PACIFIC SALMON · MULE DEER · BLACK BEAR · BLACK-FOOTED FERRET · CATFISH · BALD EAGLE · PASSENGER PIGEON · LAKE TROUT · CARIBOU · LAKE STURGEON · PADDLEFISH

BISON

PADDLEFISH · CAROLINA PARAKEET · PORCUPINE · MOUNTAIN LION · ATLANTIC WALRUS · SEA MINK · ALEWIFE · ATLANTIC DOLPHIN · ATLANTIC SALMON · BISON

Imagine seeing American buffalo (or bison) walking through fields in New York State, or jaguars sleeping in the shade of trees in North Carolina, or mountain lions chasing prey in New Jersey. You might think these things are impossible, and today they are. But they weren't in 1492. From 60 to 100 million buffalo once roamed the plains! There were no horses on the continent then. They had all died out a long time earlier. Horses wouldn't be seen again in North America until the Spanish brought them from Europe.

Take a look at the map and see which animals lived in your part of the country. Imagine what life must have been like back then, in 1492.

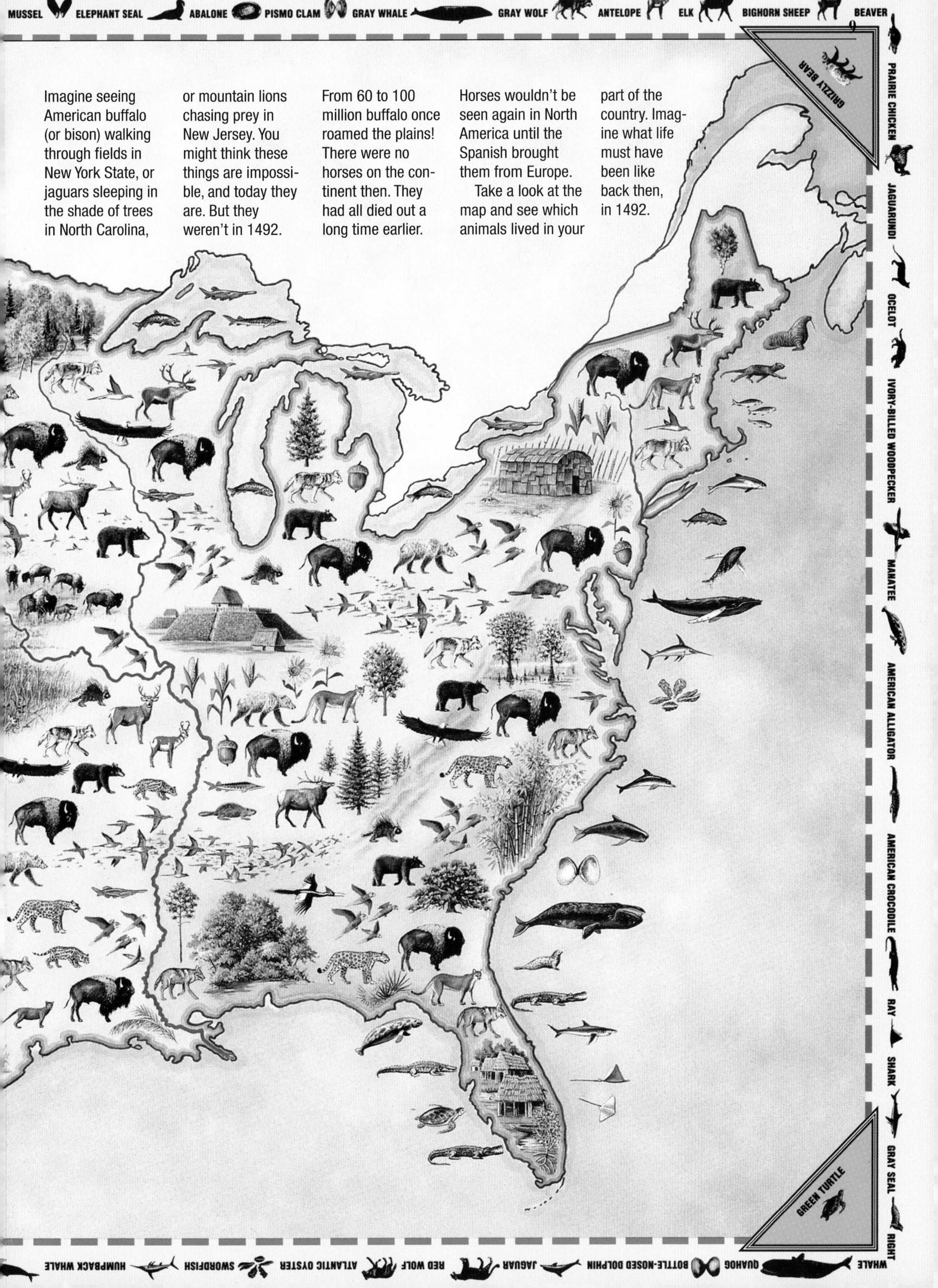
MUSSEL
ELEPHANT SEAL
ABALONE
PISMO CLAM
GRAY WHALE
GRAY WOLF
ANTELOPE
ELK
BIGHORN SHEEP
BEAVER
GRIZZLY BEAR
PRAIRIE CHICKEN
JAGUARUNDI
OCELOT
IVORY-BILLED WOODPECKER
MANATEE
AMERICAN ALLIGATOR
AMERICAN CROCODILE
RAY
SHARK
GRAY SEAL
GREEN TURTLE
RIGHT WHALE
QUAHOG
BOTTLE-NOSED DOLPHIN
JAGUAR
RED WOLF
ATLANTIC OYSTER
SWORDFISH
HUMPBACK WHALE

Eastern Woodland Peoples

Five hundred years ago, forests covered the eastern half of North America. Some early European explorers described the forests as open and parklike. That was because Native Americans cleared the underbrush with controlled burning in many areas. They also cleared fields for farming and made paths through the forest. Those paths eventually became roads and then highways.

In 1492, the Iroquois people lived in northern New York State. The Iroquois were not one people

▲ **THIS WOODEN** False Face mask belonged to an Iroquois healer. The

Iroquois believed members of the False Face society had special powers. When the members came to heal someone, they wore masks like this one. The masks gave them the power to frighten away the spirits that caused the illness.

▲ **IT'S EASY TO SEE** why the Iroquois called their homes longhouses. The buildings were 80 to 100 feet long or longer. A longhouse was shared by 10 or 12 related families. Half the families lived on one side of a long center space, while the other half lived on the opposite side. Families who lived across from each other shared a cooking fire in the center. Smoke escaped through holes in the ceiling.

Iroquois families formed clans, and there were several sets of clans within each nation. The people took part in their government by joining councils, which held meetings for making decisions. They believed in decision-making by consensus – or agreement by everyone in the council.

▲ **THE NORTHEASTERN** woodland culture stretched from the Atlantic coast to the Midwest and Great Lakes. The Iroquois nation was centered in what is now upstate New York.

but a group of five separate peoples: the Mohawk, the Seneca, the Oneida, the Onondaga, and the Cayuga. Each lived in a different area of the forest. The women did most of the farming. The men hunted and waged war. Men had to defend the villages against war parties from other groups, and they also tried to expand their own territo-ries. Boys were trained to be brave warriors when they grew up.

Right now, no one in this Iroquois village is doing any work, because everyone has stopped to watch an exciting ball game. It looks pretty rough. Let's see how the game is played.

▲ **THE IROQUOIS** called corn, beans, and squash the Three Sisters. They were always planted together, because each plant helped the other. Bean vines wrapped around the corn plants as they climbed upward. Squash vines spread everywhere, crowding out weeds. They also shaded the ground, which kept the soil from drying out. Iroquois were fond of corn cakes and corn pudding. They used corn husks to make moccasins, masks, and other items.

▲ **A WOODEN CRADLE-**board like this one made it easier for a mother to carry her baby while she did chores or traveled through the forest. The baby was wrapped in soft animal skins to keep it warm. Then it was tied to the board. The cradleboard was padded with moss to make a soft cushion for the baby.

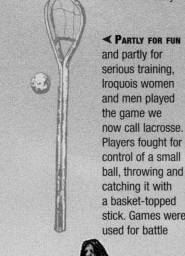

◀ **PARTLY FOR FUN** and partly for serious training, Iroquois women and men played the game we now call lacrosse. Players fought for control of a small ball, throwing and catching it with a basket-topped stick. Games were used for battle training. They could have 1,000 players per team and last several days. In such cases, goalposts were often miles apart. The players tried to hurt opposing players to knock them out of the game, and broken bones were common.

▲ **LIKE OTHER NATIVE** American peoples, the Iroquois showed great respect for the plants and animals that provided them with food, medicines, and raw materials for tools, clothing, and other things. The Iroquois hunted, fished, and gathered wild mushrooms, nuts, berries, and other fruits. When the Iroquois killed an animal, they used all of its parts. The fur or skin made clothing. Antlers and bones were fashioned into tools. After an Iroquois hunter killed a deer, he would say a prayer of thanksgiving to the animal. In the prayer, the hunter would thank the deer for giving up its life to help the hunter's people survive.

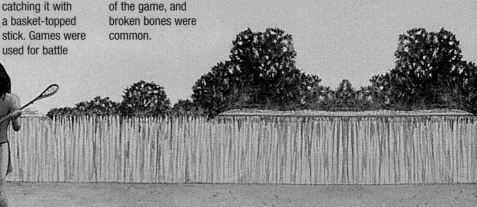

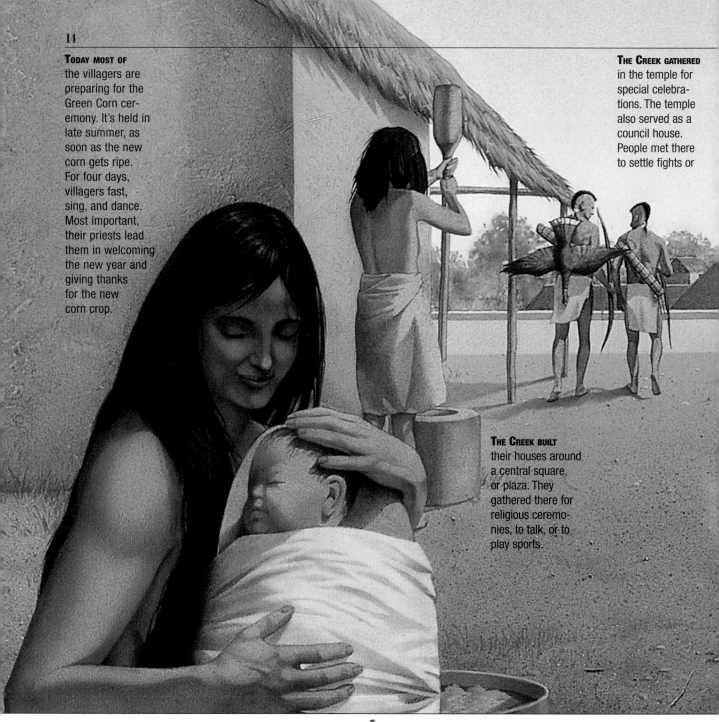

TODAY MOST OF the villagers are preparing for the Green Corn ceremony. It's held in late summer, as soon as the new corn gets ripe. For four days, villagers fast, sing, and dance. Most important, their priests lead them in welcoming the new year and giving thanks for the new corn crop.

THE CREEK GATHERED in the temple for special celebrations. The temple also served as a council house. People met there to settle fights or

THE CREEK BUILT their houses around a central square, or plaza. They gathered there for religious ceremonies, to talk, or to play sports.

Mound Builders of the Southeast

Some places where ancient peoples once lived are full of mystery. In parts of the Midwest and Southeast there are giant, flat-topped mounds of earth, some as tall as a six-story building. No one knows for sure why they were built or how they were used. Scientists do know that temples or chiefs' houses stood on the tops of the mounds. The people who made them, of the Mississippian culture, are sometimes called Mound Builders. By 1492, the Mound Builders' way of life was disappearing, but their mounds remained. New towns sprang up close by. Some of these, in South Carolina, Georgia, and Alabama, belonged to the Creek people, descendants of the Mound Builders. The Creek were farmers and hunters. They were traders too, swapping food and goods with peoples to the north and south. In this Creek village, people are getting ready for a celebration. Soon they will climb up the log stairway to the temple, and its doors will open wide. Let's find out what's inside.

to decide when to plant crops or whether or not to go to war. Creek men had to defend their villages and land from attacks by other peoples.

BOYS ARE PLAYING a popular game called chunkey. One player starts a stone disk or boulder rolling. Then all the players chase it down the court while throwing their wooden poles close to the spot where they think the stone will stop rolling.

▲ THE CREEK lived mainly in what is now Georgia and Alabama. Their name comes from their custom of settling along rivers or streams.

▼ THE TEMPLE MOUND held the sacred fire. Priests kept this fire burning from one Green Corn festival to the next. The high point of the celebration was the lighting of a new sacred fire. Everyone watched the priest put out the old fire. Then he placed ears of green corn on fresh logs and lit a new fire. After the new sacred fire was lit, the women carried embers from that fire back to their houses to light new fires in their own homes.

▼ WHEN CREEK hunters stalked deer, they often dressed in whole deerskins. In this disguise, they could sneak up on the unsuspecting animals. The Creek ate the deer's meat, saved the skin, and made tools with the bones and antlers.

➤ ▼ CREEK WOMEN planted corn, beans, squash, and other vegetables. To keep birds and animals from eating the crops, they built special stands like this (below) in the fields. Older people or young children sat on the stands, like living scarecrows. They waved their arms to drive away intruders.

Clues to the Past

How do we know that Makah girls played with toy cradles in 1492? Where did we get exact measurements for Iroquois longhouses that no longer exist? Archaeologists (ar-kee-ALL-uh-gists) find answers to such questions. Archaeologists are scientists who study ancient cultures. They look at artifacts (handmade objects) such as tools, weapons, and pottery.

Luckily, archaeologists studying Native American life in 1492 aren't limited to artifacts. They can also get answers from real people. Descendants of all the American

▼ HOW CAN WE TELL how old the objects found at ancient campgrounds are? Tree-ring dating helps. Every year, a tree trunk gets a little bigger. Each new year of growth appears as a dark circle in the trunk. A slice of tree trunk shows these rings. Scientists can tell the age of wood by counting the rings and matching them with the pattern of rings on a much older "master" tree. This makes it easier to tell the age of logs used in benches or longhouses.

THINK PIECE!

What signs of your life today do you think archaeologists will find 500 years from now? Think about the materials from before 1492 that have lasted: stone, bone, shells, pottery. What materials in your house will stand the test of time?

◄ IN THE 1930s, archaeologists found a deep pit in Colorado. It had been covered over with dirt and grass a long time ago. Inside were the bones of woolly mammoths. Ice Age hunters probably killed them thousands of years ago. To find out just how many years ago, scientists use radiocarbon dating. Bones, burned wood, and other things that were once alive contain small amounts of a substance called carbon-14, which is radioactive. It decays slowly over a long time. Scientists can measure how long the C-14 in an object has been decaying. That tells them how old it is.

Indian groups we've looked at are alive today. Hopi families still make their homes in the pueblos of Arizona. Some Iroquois people live in New York State and parts of Canada. The Mandan keep their traditions alive on a reservation and in nearby communities in North Dakota. Today, members of the Creek nation live in Alabama, Oklahoma, Louisiana, and Texas. Makah families still live in Washington State and fish in the Pacific Ocean.

Ever since the first Europeans arrived in America, Native Americans have explained their traditions to others. They're still doing that. Today, they share the ancient ways of their people with archaeologists.

◄ **MESA VERDE IS** a 20-mile-long stretch of land in Colorado. There, archaeologists uncovered a treasure from the distant past. It was the pueblos (homes) of the Anasazi. They had lived in the Southwest for about 1,000 years, until they mysteriously abandoned their pueblos in the 13th century CE. The Cliff Palace pueblo had 200 rooms.

▲ **TODAY, NATIVE** Americans continue to celebrate their rich cultural heritage with festivals. This helps them keep alive the traditions their ancestors' practiced before Europeans came.

▼ **ABOUT 500 YEARS** ago, there were heavy rains at the Makah village of Ozette. They created a mudslide that buried the village, turning it into a time capsule. Scientists know a lot about life in Ozette, because hundreds of objects were preserved almost perfectly. Scientists spent 1966 though 1981 digging through the mud. One of the things they found was this 500-year-old carved figure in a mussel shell. It matches an age-old Ozette story about the creation of life.

Storytelling

▲ **IN 1492, NONE OF** the peoples living in what is now the United States and Canada had a written language. They kept their history alive by storytelling. Around home fires and at celebrations, they told stories about where their people had come from. They also told tales about how they had lived long ago. Storytelling was a good way to teach children right from wrong. The Pueblo peoples loved to tell stories about the trickster Coyote and Grandmother Spider.

▲ **TODAY, COMPUTERS** make archaeologists' detective work easier. When researchers in New Mexico began looking for sites of pueblos almost 800 years old, they turned to computers for help. The machines analyzed thousands of maps. They found 15 forgotten pueblos. That saved the researchers hundreds of hours of work. It also kept them from making many pointless and possibly dangerous climbs up mesas and canyons.

➤ **HOW CAN ARCHAE-**ologists tell how long a longhouse was in 1492 when there's nothing left of it? One way is to study the brownish or greenish mold that grows in the dirt where wooden posts once stood. These posts held up longhouse roofs. Archaeologists sift through dirt to find the moldy stains where the holes made for the posts were. The distance between the stains shows the house's size.

Activities

WRITE A REPORT

Work with a partner or on your own. Choose two Native American groups you have read about in this magazine. Then create a T-chart to compare and contrast how the environments where they lived affected their ways of life. Include information on where their villages were located, the kinds of homes they built, the foods they ate, and how they made their clothing and tools. Use the information to write a report comparing the two groups. Be sure to include facts, details, examples, and explanations in your report. Use the magazine and do additional research as needed.

CREATE AN AMERICAN INDIAN BOOK

Suppose another class in your school is studying Native Americans, and the teacher of that class has asked you to create a book to read to the students. Work with others to write and illustrate a book about the American Indian groups featured in this magazine. Your book should include drawings, charts, and maps that describe each group's way of life. When the book is finished, make a cover that shows a map of North America with labels for each group and its region. Ask permission to share the book with another class in your school.

MAKE CONNECTIONS WITH THESE RELATED TITLES

Eastern Woodland Indians

Early English settlers approaching the coast of Carolina in ships were enchanted by the smell. One of them wrote that it felt as if they were in a delicate garden. The eastern woodlands were indeed a sweet land of plenty. Learn about the two main groups that called the eastern woodlands their home, the Iroquois and the Algonquians.

Southwest Peoples

Scorching heat, vast deserts, and little rainfall make the American Southwest sound unwelcoming to many people. But to the Native Americans who have lived in the area for thousands of years, this is cherished homeland. Learn about the Anasazi, Hohokam, and Mogollon, and their modern-day descendants, the Pueblo peoples, the Tohono O'odham, and others.

Northwest Coast Peoples

The northern Pacific coast is a beautiful stretch of land running from what is now northern California up through Oregon, Washington, and Canada. Many Native American groups settled in this region. Their sophisticated culture was marked by their spirituality and incredible craftsmanship. Learn about the daily lives and practices of the Northwest Coast peoples.

LEARN MORE ONLINE!

- No one knows for certain how the first people got to North and South America. Scientists continue to study different types of evidence, or clues, to find the answer.

- Totem poles are a feature of the Pacific Northwest peoples' culture. These standing cedar logs are carved with animal or spiritual figures and then painted in bold colors.

- Luci Tapahonso is a professor at the University of Arizona and one of the most honored poets of the Navajo nation. She spoke Navajo as a child before she learned English. She often writes her poems in Navajo and then translates them into English.

- The culture of the people of the Great Plains was centered on the buffalo. Every part of the animal was used.

KIDS DISCOVER

Houghton Mifflin Harcourt

hmhco.com

EDITOR: Jennifer Dixon
ART DIRECTION: Hopkins/Baumann, Brobel Design
DESIGNERS: Ian Brown, Ed Gabel, David Ricculli, Jeremy Rech
PHOTO RESEARCH: Ted Levine, Elisabeth Morgan, Sheila Sarmiento
ACTIVITIES WRITER: Marjorie Frank
PROOFREADER: Amy Handy

FACT-CHECKER: Nayda Rondon, Patricia Fogarty

AUTHOR: Linda Scher, Amy K. Hughes
AUTHOR TEAM LEAD: Amy K. Hughes

PRESIDENT AND CEO: Ted Levine
CHAIRMAN AND FOUNDER: Mark Levine

GRADE 5 TITLES

Regions of North America
Eastern Woodland Indians
Plains Indians
Southwest Peoples
Northwest Coast Peoples
America 1492
Exploring the Americas
Early Settlements
13 Colonies
Declaration of Independence
American Revolution
Revolutionary Women
George Washington
Thomas Jefferson
Benjamin Franklin
The Constitution
American Government
The New Nation

Lewis and Clark
Westward Expansion
Pioneers
Industrial Revolution in America
Immigration
Civil War
Underground Railroad
Postwar Change and Growth
Early 20th Century in the U.S.
Teddy Roosevelt
Suffragists
World War I
Inventors and Inventions
Great Depression
World War II
Mid-20th Century in the U.S.
Civil Rights
Into the 21st Century

ON THE COVER: Native peoples of North America, 1873. **Getty Images: Print Collector.**

PICTURE CREDITS: Art Resource, NY: HIP: p.5 center middle (Makah robe), p.5 center middle (Chilkat blanket); Smithsonian American Art Museum, Washington, D.C.: p.13 center middle (Iroquois cradleboard). **Getty Images:** Blaine Harrington III: p.17 top left (Zuni person); Breckeni: p.2 bottom right (Clovis points); Buyenlarge: p.6 center middle (Hopi woman); Culture Club: p.6 center middle (Hopi basket); George Catlin: p.8 top center (Mandan Buffalo Dance); Print Collector: p.12 top left (Iroquois False Face mask); Richard A. Cooke: p.17 center middle (Makah figurine); The New-York Historical Society: p.14 bottom center (tomahawk). **Granger Collection, NYC:** p.8 top center (Mandan lodge), p.8 bottom right (Mandan buffalo dancer); George Catlin: p.15 bottom right (Creek woman); John White: p.17 bottom center (Algonquian village); John White: p.19 top right (Algonquian village). **iStock Images:** alisafarov: p. 13 top left (bean soup mix); duncan1890: p.8 top left (Mandan chief), p.17 top right (storytelling); GROGL: p.4 bottom left (Haida canoe); Ivanastar: p.7 top left (Hopi kachina doll); LICreate: p.16 middle left (pine tree); Nicoolay: p.9 top right (bull boats). **NASA:** John C. Stennis Space Center: p.17 middle right (computer mapping). **Science Source:** James King-Holmes: p.16 bottom center (carbon dating). **Shutterstock:** Abbie: p.13 top right (whitetail buck); Doug Meek: p.16 center middle (Mesa Verde National Park, Colorado); Elsa Hoffmann: p.5 top right (seal); Mogens Trolle: p.5 top left (gray whale); Morphart Creation: p.2 center middle (ground sloth); SF photo: p.12 top center (Iroquois longhouse); Tony Campbell: p.15 bottom center (white-tailed deer); WorldStock: p.19 bottom (totem poles); Zack Frank: p.7 top right (kiva). **The Smithsonian Institute:** Paul M. Breeden: pp. 10–11 (U.S. wildlife distribution 1492).

ORIGINAL ILLUSTRATIONS:
Acme Design: Locator Maps, p.4, p.6, p.8, p.12, p.15; Cedar Box, p.5; Corn, p.6. Plant, p.7; Dog, p.9; Lacrosse Stick, p.13; Green Corn Festival, p.15; Woman Scarecrow, p.15

Brobel Design: Map of North American Land Bridge, p.3.

Wood Ronsaville Harlin, Inc.: Karen Barnes: The First Americans, pp.2–3, Mound Builders, pp.14–15; Greg Harlin: Sea People, pp.4–5; Will Williams: Buffalo Hunt, pp. 8–9, Eastern Woodland Peoples, pp.12–13; Rob Wood: Peoples of the Desert Southwest, pp.6–7.

ISBN 978-1-328-81841-6

5

1687519